100 BIBLE STORIES

of Angels, Miracles and Heaven

Marie D. Jones

Publications International, Ltd.

Signs

Therefore the Lord Himself will give you a sign: Behold, the virgin shall conceive and bear a Son, and shall call His name Immanuel. Curds and honey He shall eat, that He may know to refuse the evil and choose the good.

—Isaiah 7:14–15

You've heard the quote about making lemons out of lemonade. But did you know that God is also giving you signs—that you might make miracles out of them? The thing is, God is always around, but he only shows his presence to us in a way that comes as a sign. Have you ignored any signs lately that may have led you to a better life or helped you solve a problem that you've  been grappling with? A miracle won't unfold in your life unless you first see the key God is handing you—the key that opens the door to his guidance, wisdom, and blessings.

GOD IS OUR SHIELD

Then the LORD said to Moses, "Stretch out your hand toward heaven, that there may be hail in all the land of Egypt—on man, on beast, and on every herb of the field, throughout the land of Egypt." And Moses stretched out his rod toward heaven; and the LORD sent thunder and hail and fire darted to the ground. And the LORD rained hail on the land of Egypt.

—Exodus 9:22–23

God protects us from all things under heaven that are against us. Of course, we must first reach out and ask for that protection in prayer, but he always listens and provides us with the strength, courage, and resourcefulness to meet and overcome obstacles. It is almost like we are protected by a superhero—only the superhero is really the loving God who cares for us and stands behind us as we make our stand against our enemies. God is our shield. We need no other weapon but his presence and his love, no matter what challenges we meet along the way.

AN ABUNDANCE OF GOOD THINGS

3

Therefore may God give you
Of the dew of heaven,
Of the fatness of the earth,
And plenty of grain and wine.

—Genesis 27:28

There is always enough to go around in God's world. No need for greed, or to fight for food, shelter, and the simple basic needs, for God has generously given us the abundance of all good things if we but ask for them in gratitude and joy. The fatness of the earth is ours, and the dew of heaven nourishes us and keeps us happy, healthy, and whole. Everything we want is already here, laid out at our feet like the Kingdom of Heaven Jesus spoke of. We just have to open our hearts to recognize it, receive it, and be thankful for it.

THE ANGEL IS YOU!

4

But Moses said to God, "Who *am* I that I should go to Pharaoh, and that I should bring the children of Israel out of Egypt?"

—Exodus 3:11

Angels don't always have to be from heaven and have wings and halos and hearts of pure spun gold. In fact, you can be an angel yourself and so can the person standing next to you. God blesses each of us with the ability to help others. Consider how often you might have been an angel to someone who needed your help. In the crazy busyness of life, never miss the opportunity to be a blessing to someone you come in contact with. Who are you to be such an angel? You are a child of God and his presence is with you. It flows through you to everyone you meet. Be an angel to someone today.

ALL WE NEED TO KNOW

5

Yours, O LORD, *is* the greatness,
The power and the glory,
The victory and the majesty;
For all *that is* in heaven and in earth *is Yours;*
Yours *is* the kingdom, O LORD,
And You are exalted as head over all.

—1 Chronicles 29:11

When we recognize the one true power in our lives, everything changes. When we acknowledge God as the greatest, the one above all, the one we turn to for all our problems and needs, we realize that nothing is beyond our reach, not even the heavens. The majesty and glory of life becomes ours when we walk in the glowing light of the brightest lamp. God holds that lamp and directs our path. We may not be actual kings, but the kingdom belongs to us nonetheless, for in God's eyes we are precious royalty, meant to walk in abundance and prosperity and joy. God is great. God is glorious. God is all we need to know.

GOD HEARS THE HUMBLE PRAYER

If My people who are called by My name will humble themselves, and pray and seek My face, and turn from their wicked ways, then I will hear from heaven, and will forgive their sin and heal their land.

—2 Chronicles 7:14

Do you often find yourself wondering if God ever hears your prayers? Perhaps he is so far removed from where you are that he cannot hear your needs and your desires? Perhaps he does not care? The truth is far from that, for God in his heaven not only hears you, but always loves, forgives, and cares, no matter what your sins may be, when you turn to him in humility. It may sometimes seem as though your prayers go unanswered, but know that God's plan is not always immediately visible and understandable. If you go to him with a humble heart and offer up your prayer, you will be heard and healed.

WHEN THE TIME IS RIGHT

In the six hundredth year of Noah's life, in the second month, the seventeenth day of the month, on that day all the fountains of the great deep were broken up, and the windows of heaven were opened.

—Genesis 7:11

Nobody likes to wait for things. Waiting in line, waiting in a doctor's office, waiting for a friend to show up, waiting to hear good news, or even to hear bad news. We hate waiting. But imagine waiting as long as Noah did for the end of the Great Flood and the beginning of something new and wonderful. God's timing is rarely our own. Be patient while waiting on God. Know that he will deliver what we are waiting for when the time is truly right for us to receive it. Rather than feeling anxious and worried, we should learn to accept that when it is ready to happen, God will make it happen.

BE PROUD IN YOUR BELIEF

8

For whoever is ashamed of Me and My words in this adulterous and sinful generation, of him the Son of Man also will be ashamed when He comes in the glory of His Father with the holy angels."

—Mark 8:38

Why are we afraid to stand up for our belief in God? We seem ashamed to tell others that we rely on a higher power in heaven to help us and comfort us. Rather than being ashamed, we should thank, revere, and adore God. When we turn away from the fear and doubt and chaos all around us, we find within a silent place of peace. We know that God is there, just as he always was, and always will be. That is his gift to us.
It is a gift we should be proud of and encourage others to find within themselves as well. What a better world this would be if we all stood firm in our belief in a power greater and grander than we could ever be!

INFINITE AND UNCEASING

9

But who is able to build Him a temple, since heaven and the heaven of heavens cannot contain Him? Who *am* I then, that I should build Him a temple, except to burn sacrifice before Him?

—2 Chronicles 2:6

Just as the heavens cannot contain the power and glory of God, our hearts cannot contain all the love he has for us, for it is infinite and unceasing. That is as good a description as any of heaven right here on earth. To walk in the light of a love that

never ends is to live in a state of constant grace. Even when problems arise, that never-ending love and grace sustains us and helps us find the solutions we seek. Living in an awareness of God's presence is a heavenly feeling. It inspires and empowers us to be the best we can be, always do his will, and honor him in body, mind, and spirit.

GOD'S GOOD TREASURE

The LORD will open to you His good treasure, the heavens, to give the rain to your land in its season, and to bless all the work of your hand. You shall lend to many nations, but you shall not borrow.

—Deuteronomy 28:12

Lack of anything, whether it's love, money, support, or success, is simply failing to open your eyes wide enough to see the treasure you are surrounded by. Perhaps to see God's treasure, your eyes are not enough. Perhaps it requires looking with your faith and your heart and your spirit. God's good treasure is all around you and always has been. That is a promise he has made to you, but you must have the discerning eyes to see this treasure. You lack for nothing but the faith required to receive the bounty that already is spread out before you. You have need of nothing when you realize that all under heaven is *yours*!

Heavenly Promises of Joy

I know also, my God, that You test the heart and have pleasure in uprightness. As for me, in the uprightness of my heart I have willingly offered all these *things*; and now with joy I have seen Your people, who are present here to offer willingly to You.

—1 Chronicles 29:17

Heaven is not necessarily somewhere we go. It can be a state of mind and a sense of joy that occurs when we live according to what is right and good and true. When we follow our hearts and listen to God's guidance, we can achieve a state of heaven right where we are standing. We experience the joy of being the best we can be and of giving love to those who need it. We understand the

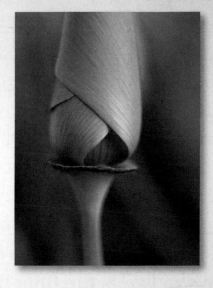

happiness that comes from serving God and giving our gifts to the world. Heaven is indeed a place we aspire to, but it is also a state of being we can enjoy right here where we are.

TRUE AUTHORITY

And Jesus came and spoke to them, saying, "All authority has been given to Me in heaven and on earth."

—Matthew 28:18

The only authority we need is that which comes to us from God. We may have power here on earth and feel like we are capable of doing whatever we want, but when we have the blessing of God upon us, all of heaven and earth are open to us. Real power that comes from God is all we truly need, and real approval from him is the only acceptance we should seek. The ways of the world are not the ways of God. The understanding that there are higher ways to live is the impetus for real growth and transformation. God's power, when given to us, supersedes all other power and places us in a position of true authority.

ALPHA AND OMEGA

"I am the Alpha and the Omega, *the* Beginning and *the* End, the First and the Last." Blessed *are* those who do His commandments, that they may have the right to the tree of life, and may enter through the gates into the city.

— Revelation 22:13–14

From the beginning to the end, God is there. He is everywhere at all times and always right where we are. His kingdom of heaven is promised to us if we do his work, live by his commandments, love others, and practice patience, tolerance, and kindness. Remember the Golden Rule? If we treat others as we wish to be treated, we will find that the gates of heaven are opened to us in the next life. But we must first practice those commandments. Our deeds, not just our words, must show that we have integrity and compassion. Then we can enter that kingdom and enjoy its blessings.

THE DIVERSE GIFTS OF GOD

There are diversities of gifts, but the same Spirit. There are differences of ministries, but the same Lord. And there are diversities of activities, but it is the same God who works all in all.

—1 Corinthians 12:4–6

What is it that you do better than most of the people you know? What are your gifts, your talents, your unique quirks and characteristics? There is no limit under heaven to what you can do and how many people you can touch by just being yourself, when you know that you do things in the spirit of love and service. What you have to give may be something that no one else can provide. Not letting that light out will deprive so many people of the positive influence of your presence in their lives. As long as you operate from the spirit, all you are and all you have is a blessing to the world.

Written in Heaven

"Behold, I give you the authority to trample on serpents and scorpions, and over all the power of the enemy, and nothing shall by any means hurt you. Nevertheless do not rejoice in this, that the spirits are subject to you, but rather rejoice because your names are written in heaven."

—Luke 10:19–20

Your name is written somewhere in a very special place in heaven, identifying you as a child of a loving and powerful God. How great is it to know that you're given such authority by the one above all others? But you must use this authority for good, and for the good of others, even those people you cannot stand and consider your worst enemies. God asks for our faith. He also asks for our ability to show empathy, compassion, and love—not just for our friends, but also for our enemies. Ask yourself if you are using your God-given authority for the betterment of humanity and not just for your own selfish purposes.

16
ANGELS IN TRAINING

"Take heed that you do not despise one of these little ones, for I say to you that in heaven their angels always see the face of My Father who is in heaven."

—Matthew 18:10

Children are filled with the magic of angels. Yet we look down upon them as being, well, childish. But when we become like children again, looking with eyes of wonder and faith, we see a world that is filled with goodness, love, and miracles. The eyes of a child are not jaded or bitter with experience. A child's eyes are windows to a life colored by God's greatest blessings. Children are angels in training.

17
THE CHOSEN ONES

And He will send His angels with a great sound of a trumpet, and they will gather together His elect from the four winds, from one end of heaven to the other.

—Matthew 24:31

We are all God's chosen. We are all God's children. He comes to us when we need him, first sending his angels to offer loving guidance. He answers our prayers when we call him, even if the answers aren't what we wanted or expected. We are God's elect. His blessings and love are available to us if we just ask for them and believe we deserve them.

GLORIOUS TO BEHOLD

18

The LORD *is* high above all nations,
His glory above the heavens.
Who *is* like the LORD our God,
Who dwells on high,
Who humbles Himself to behold
The things that are in the heavens and in the earth?

—Psalm 113:4–6

There is a magic in humility and in the ability to look at the world around us through humble and grateful eyes. We become so jaded and cynical by what life deals us that our vision becomes clouded. We miss God's heaven right in front of us. The beauty and majesty and splendor of life are often missed because our focus is on problems, challenges, and trials. Becoming humble before God and recognizing all around us his amazing creations allow us to feel that awe we once felt as little children, when everything was magical and possible and beautiful.

Worthy of the Fullness

The earth *is* the LORD's, and all its fullness,
The world and those who dwell therein.
For He has founded it upon the seas,
And established it upon the waters.
Who may ascend into the hill of the LORD?
Or who may stand in His holy place?

—Psalm 24:1–3

Just by being born we are worthy of all the love under heaven. Unlike our fellow humans, God doesn't judge us by our appearance, our job, or how much money we make. God

judges us according to the love in our soul and the compassion we give to others. When we come up short, he loves us and accepts us anyway. As long as we are striving to be better and do better, God approves and finds us worthy of having a life filled with joy, happiness, and prosperity. How awesome it is to know that we don't have to jump through hoops and be something we aren't to get God's love! It's ours to have, always.

Heavenly Wisdom

But the wisdom that is from above is first pure, then peaceable, gentle, willing to yield, full of mercy and good fruits, without partiality and without hypocrisy.

—James 3:17

We are surrounded by people who are willing to give us advice and offer their personal wisdom. We know they are trying to help, but sometimes the best thing we can do is quiet the outside chatter and turn to that still, small, inner voice that is all-knowing and all-wise. The Lord's wisdom comes from a much higher perspective than any human understanding. He can always see the bigger picture. Turning to God for the guidance and direction we need will always lead us to the best outcome because he speaks to us of a truth that only the heart and spirit can recognize.

A REFLECTION OF HEAVEN

Then God said, "Let the waters abound with an abundance of living creatures, and let birds fly above the earth across the face of the firmament of the heavens."

—Genesis 1:20

Here on earth, we are reminded every day of the amazing abundance of life around us. We see in nature a reflection of the heavenly abundance promised to us from God. From the creatures of the sea, to the birds in the sky, to the blades of grass in just one small field, we are surrounded with plentiful proof that God provides. God is right here, where we are, immersed in beauty and bounty and blessings so vast and varied it takes our breath away. Should we ever feel alone and impoverished in spirit, nature reminds us that we live in a heaven on earth.

FAITH IS THE KEY

"Also I say to you, whoever confesses Me before men, him the Son of Man also will confess before the angels of God. But he who denies Me before men will be denied before the angels of God."

—Luke 12:8–9

God offers us everything—if only we believe in him. Faith gives us access to angels who can guide and protect us from harm too, if we believe in them. This requires stepping beyond the comfort zone of only believing in what we can see and

touch and hear. God and his angels demand our faith. Why shouldn't they? Our reward in return is to know that we are always loved by him. We are also aided by the heavenly army he sends to stand beside us through the battles and challenges of life. There is no shame in having faith and believing in what cannot be seen. That faith is our power and the key to God's entire kingdom.

NO GREATER POWER

23

Oh, Lord, GOD, You have begun to show Your servant Your greatness and Your mighty hand, for what god *is there* in heaven or on earth who can do *anything* like Your works and Your mighty *deeds*?

—Deuteronomy 3:24

We can do so much on our own, and together we can do even more. But God alone can do it all, and when we are aligned with God, anything is possible. This includes the most amazing and miraculous deeds. As human beings, we've been blessed with strong bodies, minds, and spirits. We have the ability to achieve so much good, especially when we have  God working with us and for us, because there is no greater power for good in all of heaven and earth. Knowing this gives us the sense that we are always being directed, guided, and watched over by the mighty hand of God. He always points the way, even when we feel lost and alone.

LISTEN!

See that you do not **refuse** Him **who** speaks. For if they did not escape who refu**s**ed Him **who spoke** on earth, much more *shall we not escape* if we **turn** away from Him who *speaks* from heaven.

—Hebrews 12:25

When God t... How often do we ... the voice of God w... saying do this or don... this way and not that? W... call it all kinds of things like "intuition" or "the higher voice," but it's really just God telling us what we need to know to handle a **situation** or solve a problem. Imagine having a best friend and constant companion always at our side to keep us on the right track at all times. That is what the voice of God within us is—a constant companion that knows what is best for us, even when we don't know it ourselves.

ON THINGS ABOVE

If then you were raised with Christ, seek those things which are above, where Christ is, sitting at the right hand of God. Set your mind on things above, not on things on the earth. For you died, and your life is hidden with Christ in God.

—Colossians 3:1—

Focus is everything. When we focus on the things of the earth and have tunnel vision about our lives and our problems, we often miss the hidden life that is available to us if we aim our focus a bit higher. By shifting our attention to God and his purpose for us, we are transported to higher ground. Here we can see the many options and opportunities that we missed because of our limited perspective. Our minds are powerful tools. Using them to keep focused on the higher things, the things God wants of us and allows that hidden and joyful life to unfold right before our

LISTEN!

See that you do not refuse Him who speaks. For if they did not escape who refused Him who spoke on earth, much more *shall we not escape* if we turn away from Him who *speaks* from heaven.

—Hebrews 12:25

When God talks, we should listen! How often do we completely ignore the voice of God within that is saying do this or don't do that, go this way and not that? We may call it all kinds of things like "intuition" or "the higher voice," but it's really just God telling us what we need to know to handle a situation or solve a problem. Imagine having a best friend and constant companion always at our side to keep us on the right track at all times. That is what the voice of God within us is—a constant companion that knows what is best for us, even when we don't know it ourselves.

ON THINGS ABOVE

If then you were raised with Christ, seek those things which are above, where Christ is, sitting at the right hand of God. Set your mind on things above, not on things on the earth. For you died, and your life is hidden with Christ in God.

—Colossians 3:1–3

Focus is everything. When we focus on the things of the earth and have tunnel vision about our lives and our problems, we often miss the hidden life that is available to us if we aim our focus a bit higher. By shifting our attention to God and his purpose for us, we are transported to higher ground. Here we can see the many options and opportunities that we missed because of our limited perspective. Our minds are powerful tools. Using them to keep focused on the higher things, the things God wants of us and for us, allows that hidden and joyful life to unfold right before our eyes.

STATE OF GRACE

What is man that You are mindful of him,
And the son of man that You visit him?
For You have made him a little lower than the angels,
And You have crowned him with glory and honor.

—Psalm 8:4–5

When God made the angels, he made them one step above us so we would always have something to aspire to. Though we are imperfect, we can choose to be like the angels and offer love, care, and compassion to others as they would. This brings us one step closer to that perfection we aspire to. Angels serve as mentors, guides, teachers, and role models for how we can act in the world and be of service to others and to God. We may never reach perfection, but there will always be an angel nearby to help us keep striving for that state of grace in which we become angels to those around us.

MADE OF HEAVEN

The first man *was* of the earth, *made* of dust; the second Man *is* the Lord from heaven. As *was* the *man* of dust, so also *are* those *who are made* of dust; and as *is* the heavenly *Man*, so also *are* those *who are* heavenly.

—1 Corinthians 15:47–48

From dust we were created, and to dust we will return. We are of the earth, but God is of the heavens. Yet we are told that if we learn to walk in his ways, we too can become like God and overcome the limitations of an earthly life. To do this, we must have discipline and courage, because more will be asked and expected of us. Making the commitment to walk in the ways of the Lord means hard work, not always getting what we want, and doing his will rather than our own. Our human stubbornness may get in the way, but if we stay strong we will reap the heavenly benefits.

OUR EVERLASTING PROTECTOR

I cried to the LORD with my voice,
And He heard me from His holy hill.
I lay down and slept;
I awoke, for the LORD sustained me.

—Psalm 3:4–5

We often think of God as being this presence up in heaven, far away from us and detached from our problems and needs. But the truth is, God is always closer to us than our own breath and cares deeply about each and every one of us.

GOD IS AWESOME

And he was afraid and said, "How awesome *is* this place! This *is* none other than the house of God, and this *is* the gate of heaven!"

—Genesis 28:17

Too often you may focus on your small place in the world. Once you open your eyes to the majesty all around you, you'll begin to feel God's grandeur. Something wonderful happens when you step outside your existence and consider the bigger picture. You can't help but notice the magic of the world. Life is filled with ways to discover that God is awesome. You are standing before the gates of heaven right in your own backyard.

LOVE NEVER FAILS

Love never fails. But whether *there are* prophecies, they will fail; whether *there are* tongues, they will cease; whether *there is* knowledge, it will vanish away.

—1 Corinthians 13:8

Throughout your life, people will come and people will go. Friendships and relationships will start and they will end. Love will enter and love will exit. Your heart will break and be healed and then break again. But one thing remains constant: God has a steadfast and unceasing love for you. He never changes or leaves, he will never break your heart, and he will never abandon you. The love of God is the one true love you can count on for all of eternity. You can count on it even when all else is long gone and turned to dust. The inner emptiness that no person or thing could ever fill is meant to be filled by the greatest love of all, the love of God.

THE REWARD OF INTEGRITY

But You, O Lord, be merciful to me, and raise me up,
That I may repay them.
By this I know that You are well pleased with me,
Because my enemy does not triumph over me.
As for me, You uphold me in my integrity,
And set me before Your face forever.

—Psalm 41:10–12

What does it mean to have the kind of integrity that allows us to overcome evils and temptations and to triumph over challenges? Integrity is having what is inside of us, our beliefs and thoughts, match our outside behaviors and actions. God knows what we are thinking and feeling, so if we pretend to be one thing on the outside and another on the inside, we are fooling no one. God asks us to have integrity. He knows this teaches us to be responsible for all of our actions in the world and to keep our thoughts on the right things. When we walk in integrity, no enemy can knock us down. We are strong, inside and out.

WINGS OF PROTECTION

No evil shall befall you,
Nor shall any plague come near your dwelling;
For He shall give His angels charge over you,
To keep you in all your ways.

—Psalm 91:10–11

It is wonderful to know that when God cannot be there, he sends his angels to watch over us. We know that God is always with us, but how great is it to also know that his angels are watching over us, guiding us, and looking after us as well? We are so protected! Whether we have our own personal angel we like to pray to and talk with, or a special guardian angel we turn to for help during the toughest of times, we bask in the warm and comforting glow of angelic love every moment of every day. God does not want us to feel alone. We are held close under wings of protection.

WATCHING FROM ON HIGH

So then, after the Lord had spoken to them, He was received up into heaven, and sat down at the right hand of God. And they went out and preached everywhere, the Lord working with *them* and confirming the word through the accompanying signs.

—Mark 16:19–20

*I*t's easy to do good things in the world when we know someone is watching us. But can we be accountable to God and God alone? Once we learn to do the right thing even if no one is around to see it, we become the kind of

person God celebrates. We become someone who has true character all the time. Our behavior comes to reflect our love of God. We don't want to do wrong even if we could get away with it. God watches us from on high, but he encourages us to behave in the best way possible no matter what. He knows this builds our character and makes us into better human beings.

NEVER SELL YOUR SOUL

For what profit is it to a man if he gains the whole world, and loses his own soul? Or what will a man give in exchange for his soul? For the Son of Man will come in the glory of His Father with His angels, and then He will reward each according to his works.

—Matthew 16:26–27

Life hands us so many opportunities to do the right thing. But it also hands us many chances to do the wrong thing. That's why God sends us his angels. They help us make the best choices and decisions that will help us avoid doing things we will later regret. That angelic guidance tells us to hold on to what is precious and to keep it pure and good. But we are willful and are often too stubborn to listen. We sell ourselves out for what we think we want, only to find that it wasn't what we needed at all. Listen to the guidance of angels. Hold fast to what is dear and good and pure.

Messengers of God

But when He again brings the firstborn into the world,
He says:
"Let all the angels of God worship Him."

—Hebrews 1:6

Angels are messengers of God, bearing his wisdom, grace, mercy, and love. They often bring his guidance and knowledge for a very specific challenge we are facing. If we ignore the messenger, we don't get the benefit of the message. By denying the messenger, we are left to deal with our problems alone, often with a very limited perspective. We are so blessed to have opportunities to allow the angels to intercede and lead us back to God's will. Yet that cannot happen if we don't recognize them as the miraculous messengers they are. Angels are touched by the hand of the highest and sent with the love that never fails.

GUIDANCE FROM ABOVE

Now when they had departed, behold, an angel of the Lord appeared to Joseph in a dream, saying, "Arise, take the young Child and His mother, flee to Egypt, and stay there until I bring you word; for Herod will seek the young Child to destroy Him."

—Matthew 2:13

We read in the Bible of amazing stories about angels appearing before mortal men and women—people just like us—and giving them guidance, information, and instructions. Sometimes the angels even save their lives. We are no different from the men and women of the Bible. Angels speak to us each day. But their voices are in soft whispers that must be heard by the heart and the spirit. If we need guidance or help, all we have to do is ask for it, listen for the answers, and take the actions we are inspired to take. That inspiration is the urging of our angels to go where they lead us.

GOOD WORKS LEAD TO MIRACLES

Therefore He who supplies the Spirit to you and works miracles among you, *does He do it* by the works of the law, or by the hearing of faith?—just as Abraham "believed God, and it was accounted to him for righteousness."

—Galatians 3:5–6

Our faith alone can work miracles, but how much more true spiritual power do we possess when we also take action? The good works that God inspires us to do in the world double the chances of great results and working miracles—not only in our own lives, but in the lives of those around us. We are told to walk our talk and talk our walk. This is what God wants us to do. Faith is great, but when it is backed by action it is even greater. That is the secret of integrity: matching our words and actions so that they are one and the same.

STRAIGHT FROM HEAVEN

Bless the LORD, you His angels,
Who excel in strength, who do His word,
Heeding the voice of His word.
Bless the LORD, all *you* His hosts,
You ministers of His, who do His pleasure.

—Psalm 103:20–21

We can all use a guardian angel or two. The wonderful thing is, God has plenty of angels to go around for anyone who calls upon them. We can ask our angels for strength, for courage, for wisdom, and for support. We can call on them for comfort when we feel we cannot do something on our own or aren't sure of what we should do in a particular situation. The presence of our angels is an assurance. We have a host of help at hand to smooth the rough spots of life. God has sent to us, straight from heaven, his ministers and go-betweens in the form of angels who are forever ready to stand beside us.

ANGELS IN OUR MIDST

But Mary stood outside by the tomb weeping, and as she wept she stooped down *and looked* into the tomb. And she saw two angels in white sitting, one at the head and the other at the feet, where the body of Jesus had lain.

—John 20:11–12

At the most critical times in our lives, angels will appear when we need them the most. At the darkest and most difficult moments we can face, when all seems hopeless and lost, angels will be there. Angels respond, armed with wings to hold us up and to wrap around us in comfort. Angels appear, giving us strength and courage to carry on no matter what life throws at us. Angels arrive, just at the moment when we thought we would break apart and come undone. Angels fulfill important roles in heaven. They must be where God needs them to be. They watch over his beloved ones. They remind us that we are never without heavenly support.

FROM ABOVE, HE LISTENS

40

I waited patiently for the LORD;
And He inclined to me,
And heard my cry.
He also brought me up out of a horrible pit,
Out of the miry clay,
And set my feet upon a rock,
And established my steps.

—Psalm 40:1–2

One of the greatest traits we can acquire over time is patience. God's timing is not the same as our timing, and we sometimes feel as though he is ignoring us or has forgotten us completely. In truth, there are many things happening on  an unseen level. We only see the results later. So it can sometimes feel as though life is at a standstill, especially during hard times and challenges. But there might in fact be some movement, just outside our view, that will bring us the support we need. Waiting on God's timing means having things happen as they should, not as we think they should happen. Father God really does know best!

THE GOOD AND THE BAD

"Again, the kingdom of heaven is like a dragnet that was cast into the sea and gathered some of every kind, which, when it was full, they drew to shore; and they sat down and gathered the good into vessels, but threw the bad away."

—Matthew 13:47–48

God never promised that every experience in life would be a positive one. But he did promise that he would guide us through the bad and the good and help us find the lessons as well as the blessings. We have indeed been given the kingdom, and that includes many challenges and problems that can seem negative, even hopeless. But in the end, we see that it is all part of the bigger plan God has for us. These  challenges mold and shape us into strong and resilient human beings, making us more grateful, compassionate people than we were before. God chooses the lessons, but we get to choose how we handle them.

A PLENTIFUL INHERITANCE

"Remember Abraham, Isaac, and Israel, Your servants, to whom You swore by Your own self and said to them, 'I will multiply your descendants as the stars of heaven; and all this land that I have spoken of I give to your descendants, and they shall inherit *it* forever.'"

—Exodus 32:13

We reap the benefits of what God gives to us long after we leave this earthly place. The bounty and goodness becomes that of our descendants. Our inheritance becomes our children's

inheritance. The grace we receive when we turn to God for all our needs affects and influences everyone around us, like the ripples of a pebble tossed into a pond. It spreads outward and blesses everyone we meet along the way. God's good is as plentiful as the stars in the heavens. It can never be depleted or destroyed. It belongs to us all forever. We are eternally blessed when we serve God, and so are those who come after us.

GLAD TIDINGS

And the angel answered and said to him, "I am Gabriel, who stands in the presence of God, and was sent to speak to you and bring you these glad tidings."

—Luke 1:19

The appearance of an angel in your life can mean many things. Perhaps a very special angel appears to give you good news and prepare you for some life changes that you might be feeling apprehensive about. Maybe an angel comes to you with the perfect guidance and solution to a problem that has been bothering you for a long time. Angels might even come to warn you about something  that is in your future, encouraging you to take action and pay attention. Always be grateful for the presence of angels and what they are there to tell you. They are God's treasured messengers sent to assist you in all your earthly endeavors.

AN ANGEL BY MY SIDE

The LORD God of heaven, who took me from my father's house and from the land of my family, and who spoke to me and swore to me, saying, "To your descendants I give this land," He will send His angel before you, and you shall take a wife for my son from there.

—Genesis 24:7

The Bible is filled with stories of angels helping people overcome difficult obstacles, trials, and tribulations. We are never out of options and never alone when there are angels nearby. A closed door becomes an open window when God sends an angel to help us see solutions where we thought there were none. In the most dire of times there is an angel ready to whisper guidance and support into our ears. An angel may take us gently by the hand and lead us  to new ideas and higher perspectives. From there we can solve our problems. Even though we cannot always see the bigger picture, we know that our angels can.

HELPING US HOMEWARD

So rend your heart, and not your garments;
Return to the LORD your God,
For He *is* gracious and merciful,
Slow to anger, and of great kindness;
And He relents from doing harm.

—Joel 2:13

If you make a mistake or sin, fear not. There is always the help of an angel to gently lead you back to what is right and good. Angels know what God wants from us. They are always there, as heavenly teachers, to offer their instruction and help us understand the ways of God. We have so many teachers here on earth. Why would we not have them in the heavens as well? They are there to assist us in becoming more kind, gracious, and merciful, just as God is to us. God does forgive our slip-ups and wrongdoings, but how good it is to know that the angels are here to teach us ways to prevent them and make better and happier choices!

WITNESSING HIS MIRACLES

Now the multitude of those who believed were of one heart and one soul; neither did anyone say that any of the things he possessed was his own, but they had all things in common. And with great power the apostles gave witness to the resurrection of the Lord Jesus. And great grace was upon them all.

—Acts 4:32–33

When you witness a miracle happening to someone else, it gives you newfound hope and faith that something good is in store for you as well. Sometimes seeing others happy is just as joyful and thrilling as your own happiness. God's loving grace is contagious in that way. It spreads light and joyfulness each time someone is blessed in some way. Suddenly you realize that it could be you receiving those very blessings. Sure enough, it's as if a wall that was standing between you and those blessings has been lifted away. The more miracles you see, the more you believe. The more you believe, the more you will begin to receive.

GOD IS GOLDEN

Yes, the Almighty will be your gold
And your precious silver;
For then you will have your delight in the Almighty,
And lift up your face to God.
You will make your prayer to Him,
He will hear you,
And you will pay your vows.

—Job 22:25–27

We may be broke and have but a few dollars in our wallets, but one thing that is always in abundant supply is the love of God and his angels. While our paychecks may not stretch from one month to the next, the love from above is infinite and eternal. It is also better than any treasure on earth. All the gold and silver and money in the world may buy us temporary pleasure, but the one true way to permanent happiness is through the love of God and the wisdom of the angels he sends us to help us through our days and nights. Banks open and shut down. Money comes and goes. Heavenly treasures last forever.

LADDER TO HEAVEN

Then he dreamed, and behold, a ladder *was* set up on the earth, and its top reached to heaven; and there the angels of God were ascending and descending on it.

—Genesis 28:12

There is a pecking order in heaven and here on earth. God is the most powerful and loving presence there is. But that power and love is present as well in his angels, who are sent to earth to

help us figure things out. It's not that God cannot help us. He can. But he loves to see us working with his angels, his high and holy assistants, just the way a teacher in a classroom delegates to his or her assistant teachers and parent volunteers. And like children in a classroom, we can often ask for help from those assistants and volunteers. They in turn will assist us, but also have the option of asking the teacher for the final word.

WALKING TALL

Yet I will rejoice in the LORD,
I will joy in the God of my salvation.
The LORD God is my strength;
He will make my feet like deer's *feet*,
And He will make me walk on my high hills.

—Habakkuk 3:18–19

We may not be able to soar through the heavens like the angels, but we can walk tall and proud in the light of their love for us. We can be happy and grateful for the help of our angels, who are God's greatest gift to us. We should acknowledge and appreciate how angels show up just when we are open and receptive to their help. Their love is all we really need to fly and feel light in nature. God is all we need no matter what form he chooses to express his love in, and often that form is an angel hovering just above us.

Armies of Angels

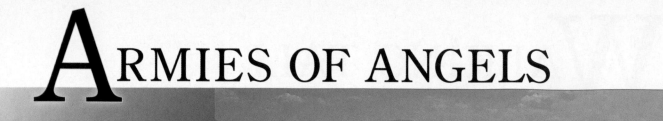

But Jesus said to him, "Put your sword in its place, for all who take the sword will perish by the sword. Or do you think that I cannot now pray to My Father, and He will provide Me with more than twelve legions of angels? How then could the Scriptures be fulfilled, that it must happen thus?"

—Matthew 26:52–54

If you are feeling as though the world is against you and everything is going wrong, remember that God has given you access to his army of angels to provide you with answers, solutions, and peace in tough times.

If you think for one second that you are on your own in this game of life, remember that God has equipped your team with his best and finest players, in the form of his mighty angels. They are ready to help you achieve victory and triumph over your enemies. Like he did with his own son, Jesus, God is ready to send down any number of angels upon request, ready to do battle for us and with us.

PURE IN SPIRIT

I charge *you* before God and the Lord Jesus Christ and the elect angels that you observe these things without prejudice, doing nothing with partiality. Do not lay hands on anyone hastily, nor share in other people's sins; keep yourself pure.

—1 Timothy 5:21–22

What does it mean to be pure—pure of heart or pure in spirit? We hear this word and wonder how we could possibly live up to the perfection it implies. But being pure doesn't mean being perfect. It means to always be striving for perfection, learning from mistakes, and desiring to grow and do better. Purity means choosing love and compassion whenever we have a choice. It means having positive motivations for our words and actions. We are pure of heart and spirit when we do our best and when we ask for forgiveness when we fall short. We are pure of soul when we keep our focus on God's love and will for us and move toward that will with joy.

WHEN THINGS LOOK BLEAK

Gideon said to Him, "O my lord, if the LORD is with us, why then has all this happened to us? And where *are* all His miracles which our fathers told us about, saying, 'Did not the LORD bring us up from Egypt?' But now the LORD has forsaken us and delivered us into the hands of the Midianites."

—Judges 6:13

There will be times in your life when things appear to be going wrong, and all looks bleak and hopeless. You'll pray, and your prayers won't be answered. You'll ask God for guidance, and you won't hear his wisdom and direction. You will feel lost, abandoned, and alone—until you remember how he has always come through for you in his own good time. God always has a miracle planned for us, but it sometimes requires our faith and patience. Maybe he is testing us to see if we are strong enough to handle the new blessings he has in store. Maybe he just knows the best times to give us what we need. Either way, God will not forsake us.

No LONGER BARREN

And he said, "Bring me a new bowl, and put salt in it." So they brought *it* to him. Then he went out to the source of the water, and cast in the salt there, and said, "Thus says the LORD: 'I have healed this water; from it there shall be no more death or barrenness.'"

—2 Kings 2:20–21

When we bring our broken hearts and spirits to God for healing, he fills us with cleansing waters. We feel renewed and refreshed and rejuvenated. How often do we not bother to turn to God for help, struggling instead to do something on our own? How often do we think we have the right answers, only to find that the still, small voice of God within was telling us we were wrong? We can be stubborn creatures.

But God is always ready to heal us and make whole what is barren in our lives if only we have the humility to set aside our human egos and our rigid ways of thinking and turn to him for help.

WE SHALL OVERCOME

54

He who overcomes shall be clothed in white garments, and I will not blot out his name from the Book of Life; but I will confess his name before My Father and before His angels.

—Revelation 3:5

Can you imagine how good it will feel to have the approval of angels before God because of the way we lived our lives? Imagine how much joy will fill our hearts when we are looked upon with love by the legions of helpers standing beside God, those witnesses to the good things we have done. If we live with the excited anticipation of being included in the Book of Life, we shall overcome all the temptations and challenges that might otherwise block us from our lofty goal. The angels are there to help us do just that. They help us keep our feet on the path that leads to God's highest reward.

EVERYONE IS AN ANGEL TO SOMEONE

The LORD has established His throne in heaven,
And His kingdom rules over all.
Bless the LORD, you His angels,
Who excel in strength, who do His word,
Heeding the voice of His word.

—Psalm 103:19–20

You—yes, you—are an angel right here and right now. There are people in this world who look to you for love, support, guidance, and direction. You get to give of yourself to help others any time you want. You get to know the joy of God's own angels in heaven. You can live your life as a blessing to others. You can do what you can, with what you have, when you can, no matter how small or insignificant your actions might seem at the time. You can make a difference in someone's life today, right here and right now. You can be an angel to someone else even if you don't have wings.

CLEANSING STRUGGLES

The temple was filled with smoke from the glory of God and from His power, and no one was able to enter the temple till the seven plagues of the seven angels were completed.

—Revelation 15:8

The presence of angels is not always a joyful experience. Sometimes we are placed in the presence of our angels to go through a very trying, challenging, and even frightening period in life for the purpose of strengthening our souls. Angels are not always bearers of good news, although they often come to us to help us get through bad news. God has given angels authority to assist us at all times, no matter what the situation might be. Sometimes an angel is sent to straighten us out when we are following a crooked road and getting into trouble. We might be afraid of them at first, but they are there to help us, even if they need to scare us a bit first.

With all your heart

"Hear, O Israel: The Lord our God, the Lord *is* one! You shall love the Lord your God with all your heart, with all your soul, and with all your strength."

—Deuteronomy 6:4–5

*L*oving God is never a one-way street. When you recognize your oneness with God, he returns the favor by lavishing you with all the good things heaven can hold. Putting your heart and soul into God's hands is never a waste of time. It is always abundantly rewarded.

Faithful and true

Then he said to me, "These words *are* faithful and true." And the Lord God of the holy prophets sent His angel to show His servants the things which must shortly take place.

—Revelation 22:6

*T*he eyes of angels see what we cannot see. Trust them to show us the best future possible. Allow them to guide us toward the highest outcome. Listen to them when they say what we must hear. The love of angels is true, for it is a reflection of God's love for us.

HIS JOY IS OUR STRENGTH

Then he said to them, "Go your way, eat the fat, drink the sweet, and send portions to those for whom nothing is prepared; for *this* day *is* holy to our Lord. Do not sorrow, for the joy of the LORD is your strength."

—Nehemiah 8:10

What a waste of time sorrow is when the abundant joy of God's presence is always within reach. We can grieve and mourn and feel the lack in our lives, but the truth is, we have a source of unlimited strength, love, and resilience that we can rely on when we need it. Yes, there are reasons to feel grief, but we must remember that we do have access to the love of God to help us through it. We will come out of our grief more whole, resilient, understanding, and compassionate than before. There are so many things to feel grateful and even joyful about when we focus on God and let our sorrows drift away.

DAY OF DELIVERANCE

"Behold, the days are coming," says the LORD,
"When the plowman shall overtake the reaper,
And the treader of grapes him who sows seed;
The mountains shall drip with sweet wine,
And all the hills shall flow *with it*."

—Amos 9:13

No matter how bleak things may be, there is always a day of deliverance to look forward to. Everything we've been struggling with will lift and be resolved. Our trials will come

to an end. It may not seem that way now, but we will look back and see all the times God came through for us after a challenge. We will see how it changed us for the better even if at the time all we could do was complain and moan. Miracles don't just happen to other people. They happen to us too. They can happen at any time if we keep the faith and keep putting one foot in front of the other.

A LOVE EVEN HIGHER

For I am persuaded that neither death nor life, nor angels nor principalities nor powers, nor things present nor things to come, nor height nor depth, nor any other created thing, shall be able to separate us from the love of God which is in Christ Jesus our Lord.

—Romans 8:38–39

We may be grateful for all that we have, including the help of our angels, but nothing is greater than the love of God. Angels can serve as intermediaries. They guide us toward a deeper relationship with God by sending us signs and signals to keep us on the right path. God's love is the wind beneath the wings of our angels. Their love for us can be our wings as well. The angels in our lives are not meant to stand between us and God but to stand with us and help us find ways to serve and love even more  deeply. They are there to help us reap the rewards of a joy-filled life beyond measure.

DOING WHAT IS RIGHT

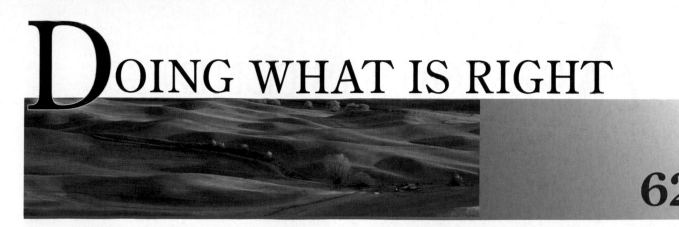

"Can a mortal be more righteous than God?
Can a man be more pure than his Maker?
If He puts no trust in His servants,
If He charges His angels with error,
How much more those who dwell in houses of clay,
Whose foundation is in the dust,
Who are crushed before a moth?"

—Job 4:17–19

Having a solid moral compass is essential to a life filled with happiness, compassion, and love. Without that compass we have no guidelines or inner directives to point us toward what is right and best, not just for us, but for those people we love and care about. We are not perfect; we need all the help we can get. This is why we often rely on our angels for that inner directive that will bring us closer to God and closer to a state of perfection. In fact, we might even consider our guardian angels our personal moral compasses, ever pointing us toward a higher and better way of being in the world.

"Which of the prophets did your fathers not persecute? And they killed those who foretold the coming of the Just One, of whom you now have become the betrayers and murderers, who have received the law by the direction of angels and have not kept *it*."

—Acts 7:52–53

When the angels speak to you, are you listening? Their wisdom and knowledge is above yours; are you ignoring their whispers in favor of the louder voice of your own mind and stubborn will? God often speaks to us directly through the angels in our lives, both the heavenly ones and the earthly ones. It is up to us to take heed of their messages and then do something with what we are told.

Can you hear your angel talking to you, or are you too distracted and busy and overwhelmed by the loudness of life? Angels often speak quietly, but their message should be loud and clear. We should listen to their soft words if we want to experience God in all his glory.

SPREADING MIRACLES

Then all the multitude kept silent and listened to Barnabas and Paul declaring how many miracles and wonders God had worked through them among the Gentiles.

—Acts 15:12

When something wonderful happens to us, we naturally want to spread the word and share it with others, to inspire them to believe that something wonderful can happen to them too. Hearing stories of miracles works a miracle in us. It

strengthens our faith and our belief that there is goodness in the world and that we can overcome the negative to find that goodness. The news may be filled with bad stuff, but the stories that affect us the most are those that empower, inspire, and move us. Stories of people being healed and uplifted serve to heal and uplift us. They allow us to be open to the miracles that exist all around us.

RIGHT THERE IN FRONT OF US

How shall we escape if we neglect so great a salvation, which at the first began to be spoken by the Lord, and was confirmed to us by those who heard *Him*, God also bearing witness both with signs and wonders, with various miracles, and gifts of the Holy Spirit, according to His own will?

—Hebrews 2:3–4

Ever notice how the answers to our biggest questions are usually right under our own noses? Ever wonder why we turn away from what could help us, as if it isn't there at all? Sometimes we ignore the obvious and pay the price for it in more suffering than is necessary. God's grace and comfort and love are right there under our noses. But do we always acknowledge and make use of it? It's time we opened our eyes and hearts to the amazing presence that is always at hand, always ready to help, and always offering a love and peace like no other. That presence is God and he never lets us down, even if we let him down.

Walking our talk

Then Philip went down to the city of Samaria and preached Christ to them. And the multitudes with one accord heeded the things spoken by Philip, hearing and seeing the miracles which he did.

—Acts 8:5–6

Many times in the Bible we read stories of people finding their faith and performing miracles. Soon others are affected and changed by those miracles. This is a chain reaction we see in our own lives as well. When people around us see

how happy we are when we put our faith in the right things, they begin to want what we have. When we walk our talk we also get to watch our own small miracles spread and grow. We see how each and every action we take influences everyone we come in contact with. We begin to watch what we say and do to make sure it is the most positive influence we can have on others.

KEEPING GOOD JUDGMENT

"*If* he has walked in My statutes
And kept My judgments faithfully—
He *is* just;
He shall surely live!"
Says the Lord GOD.

—Ezekiel 18:9

God asks us to have good judgment
and keep his rules. Is that a lot to ask
for the reward that we get in return?
He has made it so easy for us to enter
the kingdom of heaven. He has laid
out the path to real fulfillment and
happiness by simply giving us a few
rules to follow and urging us to choose
good over evil! It is hard to complain
about our place in life when God has
already given us all the tools required
to experience miracles and build a
fantastic and meaningful existence.

"What shall we do to these men? For, indeed, that a notable miracle has been done through them *is* evident to all who dwell in Jerusalem, and we cannot deny *it*."

—Acts 4:16

*I*t is hard to deny when God performs a miracle in our lives. But we do it anyway. We are human. We are stubborn. We often refuse to believe something unless we can prove how it happened and if we cannot prove it, well. . .it didn't happen. But

miracles do happen. They happen every day and not just to those who believe in them. It's as if God knows exactly where to deliver his daily miracles and just how they will fit into his plan for our lives, even when we are left clueless and wondering. God truly does work in mysterious ways, whether we can understand those ways or not. Maybe it's not our job to understand but to accept.

WATERS OF LIFE

He spread a cloud for a covering,
And fire to give light in the night.
The people asked, and He brought quail,
And satisfied them with the bread of heaven.
He opened the rock, and water gushed out;
It ran in the dry places *like* a river.

—Psalm 105:39–41

Have you ever had a thirst for something that no liquid could quench? Or a hunger for something no food could extinguish? Your spirit is what needs to be fed and given drink. The love and presence of God serves as food and drink

for a soul that is dry and weak and in need of comfort and support. You cannot buy that kind of nourishment no matter where you shop. It's only sold in one store. That store is the storehouse of love that God has given to us, his children. So drink and eat of that which will fill you up with joy—the love that only God provides.

GOD HEARS US

And may You hear the supplications of Your servant and of Your people Israel, when they pray toward this place. Hear from heaven Your dwelling place, and when You hear, forgive.

—2 Chronicles 6:21

God hears our prayers. God forgives. No matter what we have done, or where we are in life, God meets us with love and forgiveness and the chance to do things right next time. God may seem far away at times, but he is always present and always ready to forgive.

CARE AND COMFORT

Immediately the Spirit drove Him into the wilderness. And He was there in the wilderness forty days, tempted by Satan, and was with the wild beasts; and the angels ministered to Him.

—Mark 1:12–13

We are told that in the loneliest and darkest of times, God's angels will be there to minister to us. When we feel so alone and the world feels like a cold and ugly place, we can always turn to his angels for the care and comfort we need.

Merciful One

The LORD builds up Jerusalem;
He gathers together the outcasts of Israel.
He heals the brokenhearted
And binds up their wounds.
He counts the number of the stars;
He calls them all by name.

—Psalm 147:2–4

There is no break that God cannot fix. There is no wound he cannot heal. We are promised this miracle when we turn to him for help and allow God to work his wonders through us. No matter how much pain and suffering we endure physically or emotionally, God is there to offer a soothing and healing balm to what hurts. His comfort and love will hold us up as we learn to find our strength again. His care will act as sustenance for our spirits and our souls as we try to regain our hope, faith, and capacity for joy. We can and will see miracles when we let God mend our wounds.

LEARN TO ACT LIKE ANGELS

But at night an angel of the Lord opened the prison doors and brought them out, and said, "Go, stand in the temple and speak to the people all the words of this life."

—Acts 5:19–20

If we want to be like angels, we must learn to act like angels. If we want to have their wisdom and compassion, we must try their wings on for size. We must try to live as they would live. We must make choices the angels would make, take the actions the angels would take, and do the things the angels would do in order to receive the blessings of God and live a life that is full and has meaning. Learning by experience is the best way to adopt new behaviors, attitudes, and understandings. We have the constant presence of our angels to show us how we can be more like them.

THE MIRACLE OF FAITH

By faith Sarah herself also received strength to conceive seed, and she bore a child when she was past the age, because she judged Him faithful who had promised.

—Hebrews 11:11

*I*magine having access to the same miracles we read about in the Bible. Imagine being able to do what we thought could not be done. Imagine the impossible being possible. That is the wonder and miracle of having faith. When we have faith, especially faith in God, we hold within our hands a key that unlocks the greatest blessings. Possibilities surround us and we are suddenly able to see the good we could not see before because we were so focused on the bad surrounding us. Faith opens the eyes within and reveals to us that God is always giving, always good. Faith allows us to conceive the most amazing dreams and make them a reality.

GIFTS FROM GOD

For to one is given the word of wisdom through the Spirit, to another the word of knowledge through the same Spirit, to another faith by the same Spirit, to another gifts of healings by the same Spirit.

—1 Corinthians 12:8–9

How often do you take your God-given gifts and talents for granted? Yet those very gifts are what make you stand out in the world. They give you purpose and allow you to do the work God wants you to do. God gives each of us different

skills and unique talents. We should be grateful and proud of the ones we have been blessed with instead of wishing we had someone else's gifts. Some were born to teach and some were born to heal. Others were born to write, paint, build things, or lead. To hide those gifts is to hide your light. Are you hiding your light under a bushel, or sharing it with the world?

THE GOOD IN ALL OF US

Now John answered Him, saying, "Teacher, we saw someone who does not follow us casting out demons in Your name, and we forbade him because he does not follow us." But Jesus said, "Do not forbid him, for no one who works a miracle in My name can soon afterward speak evil of Me."

—Mark 9:38–39

There is goodness in all people, even when we have a hard time seeing it because of our differences. God reminds us to accept people on the merits of their character and behavior, not for which groups they belong to or how they choose to use their gifts. As long as you have a good heart and a loving soul, you are part of a much bigger group than anything humans can organize. We are human  beings with so much to offer, including the gifts of love and hope. We only hurt ourselves when we refuse to see that light in others that we wish they would see in us. God sees the light, and that may be all that matters.

Walking in Faith

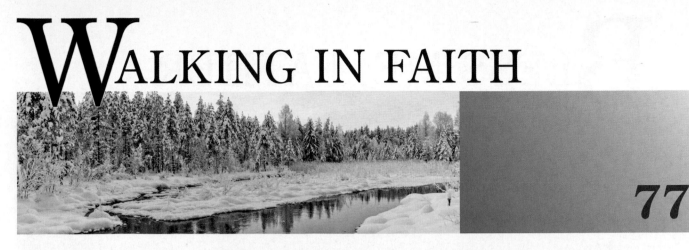

By faith Enoch was taken away so that he did not see death, "and was not found, because God had taken him"; for before he was taken he had this testimony, that he pleased God. But without faith *it is* impossible to please *Him*, for he who comes to God must believe that He is, and *that* He is a rewarder of those who diligently seek Him.

—Hebrews 11:5–6

*I*t can be very difficult to believe that good things can happen to you when all you see around you is chaos, darkness, sickness, and even death. When there are too many challenges and problems and not enough solutions and answers, it's easy to fall into the belief that God's miracles are beyond your reach and that he doesn't care. These are the times when it is most important to walk in faith and hold on tight. Often the very miracles you are searching for are just around the corner. You just have to hold on a little longer and keep putting one foot in front of the other—and have faith.

BLESS ME, FATHER

"Now it shall come to pass, if you diligently obey the voice of the LORD your God, to observe carefully all His commandments which I command you today, that the LORD your God will set you high above all nations of the earth."

—Deuteronomy 28:1

We reap what we sow. This is one of God's greatest lessons. What we send out we get back. When we act, the world reacts. When it comes to our love and faith in God, the same rule applies. If we do what he inspires and motivates and guides us to do, we reap the benefits and miracles. Otherwise, we live with great discomfort and unease, always feeling as if we took the wrong path between two that were offered to us. If we live by God's rules and word, we live a life that is simply on a higher level of joy, reward, and support than if we choose not to.

EVERYWHERE A MIRACLE

By the God of your father who will help you,
And by the Almighty who will bless you
With blessings of heaven above,
Blessings of the deep that lies beneath,
Blessings of the breasts and of the womb.

—Genesis 49:25

*I*sn't it wonderful to know that God is always at the ready when it comes to doling out blessings and miracles? No matter what our needs, he is ready and waiting to fulfill them. No matter what our hopes, he is standing by to assure us that we are loved and supported. No matter what our dreams, he has a way for us to make them a reality. God is like a father who loves his children so much that he offers them his kingdom every moment of every day. All we need to do is be grateful and accept what he offers. We will then begin to see miracles all around us, everywhere we look.

COMPASSIONATE WARRIOR

80

O God, the proud have risen against me,
And a mob of violent *men* have sought my life,
And have not set You before them.
But You, O Lord, *are* a God full of compassion, and gracious,
Longsuffering and abundant in mercy and truth.

—Psalm 86:14–15

Do you ever feel as though the entire world is against you? Do you ever wonder if anyone cares about you at all? Most of us go through times when we feel depressed, lost, and unsure about our place in the world. But God is always there. He always knows your deepest suffering. He knows how to heal it. No matter how bleak and dark your skies may appear, there is a miracle waiting just beyond the clouds. That miracle is the presence of your greatest and most compassionate warrior, your God, who will never be too busy for you.

PURE OF HEART

If I regard iniquity in my heart,
The Lord will not hear.
But certainly God has heard *me;*
He has attended to the voice of my prayer.
Blessed *be* God,
Who has not turned away my prayer,
Nor His mercy from me!

—Psalm 66:18–20

Miracles abound for those that have a heart that is pure and good. We are human, yes, and we sin and make mistakes. But if our intention is to strive to be better people and to correct our mistakes as we go along, we will keep a purity of heart that God delights in and responds to. It's hard for miracles to occur when we are filled with negative feelings and desires. It's as if we have put up a wall separating us from God's grace and miracles. But if we fill our hearts with more light, more kindness, and more compassion, that wall comes tumbling down and we are once again blessed beyond measure.

HE POWER OF BELIEF

82

But when they believed Philip as he preached the things concerning the kingdom of God and the name of Jesus Christ, both men and women were baptized. Then Simon himself also believed; and when he was baptized he continued with Philip, and was amazed, seeing the miracles and signs which were done.

—Acts 8:12–13

Believing in something that we cannot see with our own two eyes requires a deep level of faith. We often struggle to find that faith. We are so focused on being able to prove everything, but sometimes the greatest things in life are the most mysterious. When we believe, we get the joy of seeing miracles unfold every day. That's because we are looking with the eyes of possibility and promise,  and not the eyes of denial and hopelessness. Putting our belief and faith in God opens doors to all kinds of wonderful experiences. If we have the eyes and the discernment to see them, we will be able to follow the signs he leaves for us along the way.

Angels to One Another

Let brotherly love continue. Do not forget to entertain strangers, for by so *doing* some have unwittingly entertained angels. Remember the prisoners as if chained with them—those who are mistreated—since you yourselves are in the body also.

—Hebrews 13:1–3

Could that stranger who helped you out be an angel? Might that colleague who worked late with you to get a project done on time have been inspired by a heavenly force? Did that person who assisted you through a tough situation have invisible wings? God is so amazing that he chooses to distribute his angels throughout heaven and earth. His angels are often disguised as everyday people we know or strangers we've never met. Angels might even come in animal form. There are no limitations to what is possible with God. What a great reason to treat everyone around us with respect and love, just as we hope to be treated. Because maybe, just maybe, we're all angels to one another.

HEALING GIFTS

Then your light shall break forth like the morning,
Your healing shall spring forth speedily,
And your righteousness shall go before you;
The glory of the LORD shall be your rear guard.

—Isaiah 58:8

During times of illness, we often experience fear unlike any we've ever known. We may fear losing our lives. We may be afraid of losing someone we love. Fear haunts us and makes us feel helpless. But God is always there. He is like a light in the darkness or a beacon guiding us to a place of comfort and acceptance. Healings take place all the time, and a miracle is always waiting for us if we look for that beacon and follow it with all our hearts. We may be first asked to go through some very tough times, but if we follow the light, we will make it to the other side in wholeness and in joy.

GOD'S GREAT MERCY

O my God, incline Your ear and hear; open Your eyes and see our desolations, and the city which is called by Your name; for we do not present our supplications before You because of our righteous deeds, but because of Your great mercies.

—Daniel 9:18

God's mercy is one of his greatest miracles in our lives. We often equate miracles with an incredible healing or a financial windfall that arrives just in time. Yet the mercy and compassion of God is a miracle that is with us at all times.

It doesn't just happen now and then. It's always available to us when we ask for it and are open to receive it. To receive that mercy, we must humble ourselves and pray. We must ask for the signs and guidance God has to offer us. Then we must act on them. God's mercy will be our saving grace when all else seems to be lost and those more visible miracles are nowhere in sight.

86

"Behold, this is the joy of His way,
And out of the earth others will grow.
Behold, God will not cast away the blameless,
Nor will He uphold the evildoers."

—Job 8:19–20

Sometimes it may look to us like the bad guys win, but we are failing to see the bigger picture and the deeper truth. Even as we see innocent people suffer and wonder why God allows this, he is working a miracle that is happening on a level we are not privy to. God does indeed work in mysterious ways. What we judge as evil or bad might in fact have a purpose that goes far beyond our human understanding. Remember that his ways are higher than our ways. Trust him and have faith that what appears to our limited eyes to be something negative, might really be a miracle in disguise.

NEVER IN NEED

"Therefore I say to you, do not worry about your life, what you will eat or what you will drink; nor about your body, what you will put on. Is not life more than food and the body more than clothing?"

—Matthew 6:25

What a miracle it is that God always provides for us! Our basic needs are always met when we turn to God and away from fear. Our job is to have faith, not to ask how, why, or when. God will take care of the hows, the whys, and the whens.

ENDURANCE OF THE SOUL

Blessed *is* the man who endures temptation; for when he has been approved, he will receive the crown of life which the Lord has promised to those who love Him.

—James 1:12

You must overcome a lot of temptation to be blessed with God's promises. You may love God with all your heart, but your actions may be leading you down errant paths. He looks for those who can endure temptation when it crosses their path. It isn't that you'll never be forgiven, for God always forgives. But he also asks that you do your best not to need that forgiveness.

RESTORING OUR ABUNDANCE

89

"So I will restore to you the years that the
swarming locust has eaten,
The crawling locust,
The consuming locust,
And the chewing locust,
My great army which I sent among you.
You shall eat in plenty and be satisfied."

—Joel 2:25–26

The miracle of depending on God for everything we need
is that he will always provide. Even when he asks that we
accept the challenges of those lean years or when we wonder
if we have enough to survive, we must remember that we will
be rewarded with so much more. God restores to us all that
we think we have lost. He even multiplies
it so that we are overflowing with an
abundance of the things we needed.
There will even be plenty to share with
others who are also in need. Whatever
the locusts in our lives destroy, God
offers to miraculously recompense. And
he assures us that we will be taken care
of as long as we continue to walk in faith.

GOD PROVIDES

Then the LORD said to Moses, "Behold, I will rain bread from heaven for you. And the people shall go out and gather a certain quota every day, that I may test them, whether they will walk in My law or not."

—Exodus 16:4

There is always enough. We are provided for. Even when we think we have nothing, and that we are being tested with challenges, obstacles, and trials, there is enough. Just as the Lord told Moses that there would be sustenance from heaven, he also told Moses that this sustenance was reliant on how the people received it. When we receive with gratitude and make sure to spread the wealth of what we have, there is always more to fill the void. That is the way God wants us to live, with the knowledge that we are taken care of, and that we must pass the tests of faith and trust we are given in order to receive the bread from heaven God has promised.

JOYFUL GARMENTS

I will greatly rejoice in the LORD,
My soul shall be joyful in my God;
For He has clothed me with the garments of salvation,
He has covered me with the robe of righteousness,
As a bridegroom decks *himself* with ornaments,
And as a bride adorns *herself* with her jewels.

—Isaiah 61:10

*J*ust as a wedding is a joyful occasion, we also experience the miracle of joy when we celebrate God's presence in our lives. Too often we focus on the times we feel God is not there for us. We forget all the times he was there, not truly understanding that even his absence can be good for us, strengthening us and encouraging us to stand up for ourselves. That kind of tough love is just as precious as God's softer, kinder love, and both serve to empower us and help us lead more righteous lives. Rejoicing in this miracle of God's love is something we don't do enough, but when we take the time to say thank you, we are further blessed.

THE MIRACLE OF THE LOAVES

And He took the seven loaves and the fish and gave thanks, broke *them* and gave *them* to His disciples; and the disciples *gave* to the multitude. So they all ate and were filled, and they took up seven large baskets full of the fragments that were left.

—Matthew 15:36–37

Where there appears to be lack, God fills the emptiness to overflowing. Where there seems to be not enough, God takes what little we have and multiplies it. The miracle of the loaves reminds us that there is a power far beyond our own limitations that can create something out of very little when we turn to that power for help. That power is the grace of a God that wants to feed his children with the kind of food that lasts. Our gratitude for what little we have allows God to work miracles in us. He increases all the things we have to be grateful for. There is no lack that God cannot turn around and no empty basket he cannot fill.

HE WILL DELIVER US

93

"He sent from above, He took me,
He drew me out of many waters.
He delivered me from my strong enemy,
From those who hated me;
For they were too strong for me."

—2 Samuel 22:17–18

You hear a lot of people talk about being saved by God as if it only happens to the lucky few. That is not true. God is willing to help all his children if they allow him to. It's as simple as just having faith and staying strong during a difficult time. It's as simple as allowing him to work through us and others to find the perfect solution. But we have to be open to God. When other people cannot seem to help us, we can and must turn to the one who can. When our own strength and courage falls short, God steps in to remind us that we can always lean on his.

THE LORD'S FAVOR

Remember me, O LORD, with the favor
You have toward Your people.
Oh, visit me with Your salvation,
That I may see the benefit of Your chosen ones,
That I may rejoice in the gladness of Your nation,
That I may glory with Your inheritance.

—Psalm 106:4–5

Do you think you are unloved and uncared for? Do you ever feel like you are all alone in the world, even though you have friends and family? Just remember your special inheritance as a child of God and you will know that you are blessed in all ways. It's human habit to think you have been

abandoned just because your prayers are not always coming true right away or because things aren't always picture perfect. But nothing could be further from the truth. You always have the favor of the Lord, even if you don't always understand the way he delivers it in your life. Trust him. Be patient. He has chosen nothing but good things for you.

UNCONDITIONAL LOVE

95

Now hope does not disappoint, because the love of God has been poured out in our hearts by the Holy Spirit who was given to us. For when we were still without strength, in due time Christ died for the ungodly.

—Romans 5:5–6

Love often comes with a million conditions, at least here on the earthly plane. But the love of God has no conditions. We aren't required to be perfect or completely pure or to think a certain way. We don't have to do anything to be worthy of his love except acknowledge it and celebrate it. Unconditional love seems foreign to us. We look at love as something romantic or familial, and this leads to all kinds of expectations. God expects nothing except that we take his love when offered and revel in it. And when we do that, we naturally want to spread that love to others in return.

ALL AROUND US

So it was, when the angels had gone away from them into heaven, that the shepherds said to one another, "Let us now go to Bethlehem and see this thing that has come to pass, which the Lord has made known to us."

—Luke 2:15

*P*eople all over the world report seeing and interacting with angels. Though the stories may differ, the message is the same. God sends angels to help us, to guide us, and to assist us when we cannot do things for ourselves. Even though we cannot always see our angels, or speak directly to them, they are always there, watching over us.

Yet for many, angels come in material form. They appear as friends, teachers, even strangers and pets. They may be lacking wings and a halo, but we recognize the goodness and kindness and compassion they offer, and we are grateful to God for their presence in our lives. Angels are everywhere, anytime we need them.

HEALING POWERS

Now God worked unusual miracles by the hands of Paul, so that even handkerchiefs or aprons were brought from his body to the sick, and the diseases left them and the evil spirits went out of them.

—Acts 19:11–12

The miracle of healing does happen. Stories abound of people overcoming devastating disease and injury in a way that truly does seem miraculous. Have faith that these miracles can happen to anyone. Be open to the healing that comes from believing that God can bring us back to wholeness.

WILLING TO RECEIVE

Now a leper came to Him, imploring Him, kneeling down to Him and saying to Him, "If You are willing, You can make me clean." Then Jesus, moved with compassion, stretched out *His* hand and touched him, and said to him, "I am willing; be cleansed."

—Mark 1:40–41

People love to give each other gifts. But few of us are really able to receive in return. Funny how we often lack that willingness to receive good things from others. That willingness is critical, though. It opens our minds, spirits, and hearts to truly receive the gifts and miracles we are being given. There can be no giver without a receiver. To receive God's kingdom we first must get over our egos.

BLESSINGS OF HEAVEN

Ask the LORD for rain
In the time of the latter rain.
The LORD will make flashing clouds;
He will give them showers of rain,
Grass in the field for everyone.

—Zechariah 10:1

Ever count your blessings? The
funny thing is, once you do, you find
out you have more than you originally
imagined. It's as if by just focusing
on what God has provided you, the
goodness in your life is magnified. You
find that as you go through your day,
more blessings pop up, and even when
challenges arise, you feel ready to take
them on. You'll even come to see the

lessons they offer. God will open the floodgates of heaven
for you when you appreciate the things he does. Show that
gratitude daily and it will lead to more and more things to be
grateful for. Funny how it works that way.

LIKE SO MANY STARS

100

Blessing I will bless you, and multiplying I will multiply your descendants as the stars of the heaven and as the sand which *is* on the seashore; and your descendants shall possess the gate of their enemies.

—Genesis 22:17

Try counting the stars in heaven and you will know the love God has for us. That he could give us more blessings than stars in heaven and grains of sand on the beach is his joyful gift to us. Those blessings God gives us include happiness

and health for our families as well, and for all those who come after us. Each passing generation will share in the good of what God has provided. All we need to do is keep our faith directed heavenward, our hearts grateful and open, and our eyes focused on our blessings. We will continue to experience the joy of watching them increase and multiply.